The Passion Project

Dr. Chetana Rajesh

AF518721

BlueRose ONE .com
Stories Matter
NewDelhi • London

BLUEROSE PUBLISHERS
India | U.K.

Copyright © Dr. Chetana Rajesh 2025

All rights reserved by author. No part of this publication may be reproduced, stored in a retrieval system or transmitted in any form or by any means, electronic, mechanical, photocopying, recording or otherwise, without the prior permission of the author. Although every precaution has been taken to verify the accuracy of the information contained herein, the publisher assumes no responsibility for any errors or omissions. No liability is assumed for damages that may result from the use of information contained within.

BlueRose Publishers takes no responsibility for any damages, losses, or liabilities that may arise from the use or misuse of the information, products, or services provided in this publication.

BlueRose ONE.com
Stories Matter
NewDelhi • London

For permissions requests or inquiries regarding this publication, please contact:

BLUEROSE PUBLISHERS
www.BlueRoseONE.com
info@bluerosepublishers.com
+91 8882 898 898
+4407342408967

ISBN: 978-93-7018-921-8

Cover design: Yash Singhal
Typesetting: Namrata Saini

First Edition: June 2025

Foreword

This collection of poems titled 'The Passion Project' by a dedicated doctor and an aspiring poet, Dr. Chetana Rajesh, takes us through myriad paths and diverse terrains.

The collection is rich with vibrant colours of our existence, solemn music that can be heard in silence and a rhapsody that stirs up our innermost feelings as well as thoughts. It is a testimony of the emotional upheavals that one goes through and how that landscape of life transforms with the passage of time.

The poems emerge as creative pieces, replete with true reflections on the poet's journey of writing and life, to offer diverse perspectives on human experiences. Whether a poem is about solitude, loneliness, supremacy of the beauty of the loved ones; transitional nature of superficial beauty; bonding with dear ones; moments of self-doubt and so on— each piece touches the heart as a genuine revelation. The words kindle a murmuring sound waiting to be heard, understood and perhaps delved into.

The collection is a storehouse of introspective poems marked with deep thoughts, observations and feelings. The profound contemplations help readers venture into folds of human psyche and all that the poet undergoes in various stages of life.

The fine expressions, excellence in portraying different shades of life are moving and heart-warming. The collection of poems wants us to pause, give a thought and acknowledge the great influence of emotional insights, perspectives, experiences that colour the way we view the outside world and the tone within each of us.

- Dr Madhulika Singh

Contents

Safe Haven

In a crowd, often clueless,
In my own company, I find solace,
My mind is my safe haven,
And the thoughts in them, a liberating form of
expression.

Each secret stays carefully preserved,
Every stray thoght carefully reserved,
A world of my own,
A strange but cosy kind of home.

But in the midst of supposed safety,
Sudden pangs of cruel reality,
Threaten this safe haven,
And thoughts not meant for overt expression.

In a crowd, often clueless
In my own company, I find solace,
Yet, these sudden pangs of reality,
Snap me out of this dreamy epiphany.

Footprints in the Sand

Footprints in the sand,
Core memories and comfort in them,
A fear of oblivion,
Overshadowed by underlying insecurity.

Footprints in the sand,
Washed away by the fierce incoming waves,
A moment ago, filled with happiness,
And within the blink of an eye, replaced with a sense of emptiness.

Footprints in the sand,
Secrets swept away by the blue water,
A moment ago, everything was well
And within the blink of an eye, the stability of the preceding moment is lost.

Footprints in the sand,
Stay the same despite being fleeting,
Yet the whirlwind of emotions unlike the footprints,
Make the comforting one hard to hold onto.

Transition

A slow transition
Newfound inhibitions,
And with time rapidly passing by,
You wonder if true happiness is
nothing but a beautiful lie?

Traversing through unfamiliar waters,
Subtle hostility lurking in shady corners,
Every now and then though, sunshine breaks
through the clouds,
Drawing one's eye to the beauty all around.

As one navigates through the transition,
Overcoming old inhibitions only to find new ones,
Every day brings a new kind of revelation,
With the insecurities catching up,
no matter how fast one runs.

Yet in between inhibitions and hostilities,
Also exists the realm of possibility and
new-found capabilities
Because every now and then,
golden sun rays break through the clouds,
Drawing one's attention to the beauty that is around.

Rhapsody

Word speak to me,
Shaping an unsung rhapsody
The tunes of which form a reflection
Unravelling this constant need for a distraction.

Holding the power to be transformative,
Exposing the truth behind a false narrative
These tunes now form a revelation
In a rhapsody with no element of fiction.

Yet not the rhapsody,
But words are the true epiphany,
Not the tunes nor the melody,
Can truly encompass its immensity.

Because it's words that speak for me,
That turn emotions into this rhapsody,
And neither tunes not melody,
Only the power of words truly captures its immensity.

A father's love - from the daughter's perspective

Some are defined by a protective instinct,
With fierceness, others made distinctly,
Some provide the ideal shoulder to lean on,
Some restore hope when everything seems lost.

At times, their hearts may be made of stone,
Some may have left us long ago;
Some may seem more understanding,
But in the end, all of them are equally loving.

Some may share our profession,
That may seemingly increase our tension,
And some may not,
And explaining ourselves may seem like a lot.

But neither profession not their protective instinct,
It is every fathers love that makes them distinct,
And it's not always easy to understand,
Yet often, your every wish, secretly or not becomes their command.

Blue Immensities

Trying to fathom the immensity,
Four pair of eyes look across the sea,
Some reflect upon past memories,
While some anticipate future opportunities.

The blue brilliance though,
With limitless potential to grow,
Is beyond what imaginations can capture,
Leaving the most focused minds enraptured.

Yet as time continues to fly,
A realisation that so far passed them by,
Dawns upon them slowly,
One that to the heart makes this blue immensity sacred and holy.

But it's not the immensity,
Or even the brilliant blue intensity,
It's a strange sense of calm that's homely,
The peace embodied blue cheering you up when you are lonely.

Mirror

Honest about every rise and fall,
Is the mirror the hangs on the wall,
To some, just a means of seeing their reflection,
For others, merely a means for deflection.

But to me, every time I look into it,
It breaks me bit by bit,
Because the person that stares back at me,
Is not really who I want to see.

The mirror reveals the bitter truth,
Extending far beyond the petty worries of the youth,
It tells you who you are,
And uncovers your journey so well.

So, when one looks at their reflection,
From the truth, a mirror provides no deflection,
It always will reveal,
All the deep dark secrets we are trying to seal.

Silence

An unusual story,
With no real glory,
About the feelings I hide,
In my silence, they reside.

They say silence has power,
But for some it's really just a cover,
To protect them from their emotions,
Or just to help them go through the motions.

Often considered hallmark of cowardice,
While admittedly, not a harbinger of bliss.
Silence has strength,
Achieving a lot more than with talking at length.

Our emotions guide us,
Conversations may not be worth all the fuss,
I often choose to stay quiet,
Whenever unsure of the ability to do what's required.

But mostly in my life,
Through my silence I hide,
What I truly feel,
Hoping with its strength, my heart can heal

The Midst of Good Times

Often in the midst of good times,
Like the irritating alarm that constantly chimes,
But eventually even flowers cease to bloom,
And suddenly I am overcome by this sense of gloom.

It's not really a feeling of being lonely,
Not even the lack of something homely,
This kind of feeling is inexplicable,
Being overwhelmed by it is inevitable.

Not easily understood,
A kind of negativity that is not good,
But this feeling is not something I can shake,
From me, this feeling I wish, away someone could take.

Often in the midst of good times,
Like the irritating alarm clock that continuously to chime,
This feeling I'm trying to overcome;
Hopefully the path to recovery has just begun.

The Heart's Caterer

Every time I put pen to paper,
To my heart's voice I cater,
Gathering all those thoughts that seem amiss,
Immortalising both the moments of melancholy and bliss.

Something that brings me satisfaction,
Always a welcome discharge,
Like the diary into which my heart I can pour,
Where I can clearly express that desire of wanting
something more.

Even in those moments of melancholy,
A somewhat image starts forming clearly,
But often blurred by fleeting emotions;
The image turns into some form of a commotion.

And as those little fragments become whole,
A light flickers on inside my soul,
And as my emotions come to life in front of me,
Leaving me struck with a new kind of clarity.

The Smile

I look for the smile that will reach your eyes,
The kind that comes with a feeling that no one denies,
Something that touches your heart,
And renews your inner spark.

This feeling rarely does arrive,
To find it all of us strive,
But our emotions are like seasons,

Changing for the slightest of reasons.

But on days that are rare,
When there is no real burden to bear,
That smile creeps onto your face,
Allowing us to escape that tangled emotional maze.

So look for the smile that touches your heart,
Makes you feel that you have that renewed start,
Cause someone somewhere will bring to you eyes,
The smile that comes with the feeling that no one really denies.

The Walk

On a lonely walk with my headphones plugged in,
As the lights of happiness with me start going dim,
I go into deep contemplation,
This is really not an easy expedition.

And though the songs continuously change,
It never goes, this feeling that seems strange,
And as the songs try lift my mood,
It seems with me, happiness doesn't
really want to collude.

Although the walk doesn't seem long,
And nothing really seems wrong,
I am consumed by this emptiness,
Like inside me, there is an inexplicable loneliness.

Ultimately this walk will end,
But this feeling inside me won't really end,
And as life continues to be lonely,
I look for that one person or place that seems homely.

The Lost Hope

Into this sinkhole I keep falling,
Now I've stopped seeing the point in stalling,
I think it's time to accept the reality,
There is no point in further denying the actuality.

They say life goes on,
But the road has always been forlorn,
And now with no one in sight,
I have to resign myself to this current plight.

And though I know life is about moving on,
I only find myself looking back at moments long gone,
Looking on all I see are my fears,
No longer am I able to hold back the tears.

And so I let go,
Resigned that I've lost the happy glow,
Becoming my former self now seems beyond the scope,
It feels like time to let go of all hope.

The Vicious Cycle

Like that catchy song gets stuck in your head,
I am stuck in this vicious cycle that makes me feel dead,
And on and on the cycle goes,
To others, how dispensable I am it shows.

The cycle is vicious,
Rendering those caught in it delirious,
They say fortune favours the brave,
Yet this feeling many carry to the grave.

Granted that to some life is kind,
But for others, it's like their pain is being played on rewind,
And as they eagerly await a distraction,
From their grief, they hope for a retraction.

Though many say things will get better,
Even if optimism gets followed to the letter,
It rarely does being cheer,
Rather just forces us to hide every tear.

Rare Moments

A happy memory,
The rare symmetry,
At times life surprises you,
Encourages you to try something new.

Like a breath of fresh air,
Or the shade that helps one escape the sun's glare,
These moments allow you to dream,
To your eyes it brings that shiny gleam

This feeling is like that song,
Allowing you to get lost in a throng,
Those rare moments of clarity,
That makes you forget life's cruel disparity.

And to dream, those who dare,
Who posses the passion to embrace their creative flare,
These moments are just like that song,
That allows you to get lost in a throng.

Inexplicable Feelings

Words can't really explain,
The hole that burns in my heart,
Drowning in a sea that makes me insane,
Things ended before they could start.

Lying alone in bed
Ignoring the heartache
Trying to remember good times instead,
But happiness is hard to fake.

It's not that I am lonely,
Or that nothing here is homely,
Yet at times I get this feeling,
From a different kind of pain I am reeling.

Like I said words can't really explain,
This feeling makes me insane,
To heartbreak many have borne witness,
But for one's understanding, this feeling is hard to harness.

Yet life's clock continues to chime,
This feeling come without reason or rhyme,
Because on the outside, I'm surrounded by people;
But on the inside, this feeling rarely becomes feeble

Reflections of Reality

Standing in front of a mirror,
Taken over by a sudden terror,
She wishes to put herself out there,
But at her reflection, all she does is stare.

Wishing to make an impact,
Yet when with reality she come: in contact,
Her reflection is not what she wants to see,
The person looking back at her is
not who she wants to be.

So she decides it's time to make a change,
Yet she doesn't know how much emotions can derange,
With them as her guiding light,
She misses what's hiding in plain sight.

Whether in reality or reflections,
Using her emotions as deflections,
She realises her reflection is nothing but a distraction,
Enough she has in her life to have complete satisfactions.

The Idle Girl

An idle girl,
A joyous twirl,
But the eyes that saw her,
Found her queer.

Yet she remained free,
Undeterred by societal decree,
Continuing to blaze her own trail,
She was anything but frail.

But freedom has its bounds,
The irony here is profound,
They say perseverance is key,
But can one really break free?

The struggle is real,
Not everyone is made of steel,
Yet an idle girl with her joyous twirl,
Makes the freedom ideology

Heartbreak

Oh what do I do with this heart of mine,
The damn thing breaks every time,
And every time it tries to mend,
There seems to be another loose end.

And everywhere I turn,
Feel like there's no reprieve that I can earn,
And yet again tears fill my eyes,
In my heart ; all sense of hope dies.

Yet I try to pick myself up,
This feeling of emptiness I try to gulp,
Yet I can't help but wonder,
Is wanting to be happy nothing but a huge blunder.

All I'm left with really is doubt,
Contemplating all the words that have come out of my mouth,
What is my fault I wonder,
That sadness struck my life like thunder.

Insignificant

If only through my eyes,
You could see past all the lies,
And past all these masks I wear,
See me cry my every tear.

On the surface, everything seems fine,
Yet if you looked deeper into this life of mine,
The reality would become apparent,
Wish it was easier to make my thoughts transparent.

Insignificant on so many days I feel,
On such days I wonder if my heart can ever heal.
Will there ever be a day when I am better off ?
Or will I keep waiting for the day my life
will finally take off.

To all these questions, there never will be an end,
Some fences we can never truly mend,
As for life, it goes on and on,
And with it, all my days go on and on.

The New Chapter

With hope in her eyes,
And dreams to touch the skies,
She steps into this next phase,
And towards her next goal, she begins her chase.

It's a new chapter of her life,
And as she cuts through each new challenge with her sharp knife,
This new path she tries to create,
That for her forges a new fate.

But this is just a start,
Towards following her own heart,
And as the chapter changes,
For a new set of goals she arranges.

And she finally realizes,
That in every chapter, there will be many highs,
And as she turns the page,
A new dream will be released from its cage.

Pretty

As she puts on her red lipstick,
Along with her eyeliner real quick,
She looks into the mirror,
The true meaning of pretty is what she's trying to discover.

Again when she goes out to buy a dress,
Upon its colour or style she does not stress,
But each dress that she goes out to buy,
Makes her wonder if the true meaning of pretty will pass her by.

And with each passing day,
She worries about the inevitable delay
For she thinks all problems can be solved,
If the true meaning of pretty can be resolved.

But now, as her youth has gone by,
She realises with a deep sigh,
That toward being truly pretty, neither makeup nor dresses are a true start,
But the true meaning of pretty lies in the purity of one's heart.

As she puts on her red lipstick,
Along with her eyeliner real quick,
She looks into the mirror,
The true meaning of pretty is what she's trying to discover.

Again, when she goes out to buy a dress,
Upon its colour or style she does not stress,
But each dress that she goes out to buy,
Makes her wonder if the true meaning of pretty will finally pass her by.

And again with each passing day,
She worries about the inevitable delay,
For she thinks all her problems can be solved,
If, by her, the true meaning of pretty can be resolved.

But now, as her youth has gone by,
She finally realises with a deep sigh,
Toward her goal, neither makeup nor a dress is a start,
The true meaning of pretty is the purity of one's heart.

A Second Chance

Just for a moment, let's slip into a trance,
Once more let's do this dance,
And wonder what could be,
If through new eyes, the same moment we could once more see.

Once again let's revisit all those moments,
And compare them with recent developments,
So that from past mistakes we can learn,
To finally attain the perfection for which we always yearn.

But sometimes looking back at a past blunder,
I often wonder,
How can we warrant that these mistakes we won't repeat,
And indeed with a second our expectations will meet ?

But then again, optimism is the way to go,
As we can never really know what difficulties at us life might throw,
So let's forget everything and slip into this trance,
And once more let's do this dance.

Memories

Brightening my day,
With me they will always stay
In flashes they come and go,
Within the mind, these precious moments continue to flow.

Sometimes while sitting with friends,
Or while observing the changing trends,
To them the discussion always drifts,
With them, the mood always lifts.

Even when I'm alone,
Looking back at all those moments
that are now long gone,
These moments that come with a wave of relief,
Obliterating the occasional moments of grief.

Brightening my day,
With me, they will always stay.
And even though eventually many may fade,
With every passing moment, a new memory is made

Lost Opportunities

Often, decisions made in haste
Let the most treasured moments go to waste,
And as we look back at these,
One is struck by a strange sense of unease.

And as I look back in time,
Every wasted opportunity seems like a crime,
The reasons that I wasted them seem so lame,
Only now do I realise that such
opportunities are hard to tame.

But with every opportunity that I've lost,
I realise not everything can come at a cost,
Not every time can we blame the hand that we are dealt,
For sometimes, the pain of losing
someone demands to be felt.

So next time, whenever an opportunity presents itself,
And you feel that it is worth chasing yourself,
Give it your best shot,
As in the trap of lost opportunities, no one deserves to be
caught.

Struggles

I stand here all alone,
Everything I had is gone,
I have nowhere to go,
Nothing to tell and nothing to show.

On this road, there are no friends,
It's here that many dreams have met with their ends,
But to give up today, I'm not ready
And so I begin my journey, slow and steady.

Neither in the dark of the night,
Nor in broad daylight,
Does this journey become easy,
And the obstacles once again prevent
me from moving freely.

Every step does not lead to win,
There are times when all looks grim,
But through the darkness, sometimes you have to smile,
Because often it is the end that makes it worth the while.

Conflicting Worlds

My textbook lies open in front of me,
Yet my eyes drift into a world of fantasy,
Where I can be what I want to be,
Here, I need nobody's permission to declare myself free.

Again a question arises in my mind,
Will my fantasy world always remain this kind ?
And in this conflict between fantasy and reality,
I realise that in both worlds, every moment
cannot be spent with glee.

In both worlds, my dreams remain the same,
But the question remains in which world
they remain easier to tame,
However, the easiest paths are not always best,
Sometimes the mind must be put to the test.

But whether in reality or in fantasy,
There is a palpable amount of agony,
But for those who dare to dream,
To guide them, the guiding light will continue to beam.

Turning Point

There are certain moments in life,
Where we often find ourselves in a strife
And as we often contemplate whether the right decision
was made ?
That little shadow of doubt begins to plague.

It is of course at this time,
That the mind begins to chime,
And one often begins to wonder,
If at that point one has made one big blunder.

But whenever one is in doubt,
And you begin to feel that nothing is going to work out,
Just stop and close your eyes,
And try to figure out what it is that really matters in life.

For we all know that life is too short,
And thus, with sadness, we must not distort,
What can be a beautiful ride,
Must be enjoyed keeping all our worries aside.

A Mother's Journey

No longer do I see her sweet innocent face,
They say into this world, everyone enters in a haze,
Into the game of life, with all its twists and turns,
But I always taught her, with every stumble,
one only learns.

The hand that I used you hold,
Has now become aware that everything that
glitters is not gold,
And as she comes to the realization that the world's cruel,
She stands at a juncture where she's
fighting more than one duel.

Now the struggle of life knocks at her door,
And striving for success has started driving her sore,
But no longer can I go and help,
Because in life, every emotion has to be felt.

For the time I held her in my hands,
To where today, she stands,
Her mother I will always be,
And a person I'm proud of is what I see.

Of her, to this day, I continue to be proud,
And just as I promised her as a child to never
lose her to the crowd,
It is now she, who holds my hand,
And says, 'Mom, with you, I will always stand.'

Unspoken Words

Hearts are often broken,
As certain words remain unspoken,
Until it's suddenly too late,
And all is then left up to fate.

But every now and then, one is forced to think,
Why to the back of our mind, we let the strongest
emotions sink,
Is it because to express our true feelings we are afraid,
Or is it because in our expression, we are merely delayed?

Often they say " the world seems so small"
Yet as long as egos stand tall,
Communication can never truly be complete,
And of true emotions, this world we will
continue to cheat.

So next time follow your heart,
Don't hide your emotions until they fall short,
Because hearts often get broken,
When certain words remain unspoken.

Abandoned Leaves

Abandoned these autumn leaves lie,
Ignored by some who pass by
And brushed aside by the rest,
As time passes, their patience is put to the test.

Up above, their friends the trees lay bare,
For them too, people no longer care,
Because a tree that doesn't give fruit,
In man's eyes there will always be a substitute.

Despite being gold,
The story of these leaves remains untold.
Separated from their friends,
With nature, man never makes amends.

And so they lie there,
Starved for a little affection and care,
Yet no one spares them a second glance,
To nature's tune, man still does not dance.

The Golden Days

These red brick walls,
Volunteering at the heritage mela stalls,
Opening our tiffins in between classes,
Not realising how fast time passes.

And now as school comes to end,
And there are no more classes left for us to attend,
We realized how badly these golden days of
school will be missed,
I'm not yet ready for my school life to cease to exist.

And yet the time has come,
For us to step into the sun,
As teachers would say,
Now is the time when our hard work will pay.

Yet in all these years, all these unforgettable
times we've shared,
The place where we learnt that not everything
broken can be repaired,
The place where we made lifelong friends,
School's where we learnt to believe that
we can set new trends.

Most of all, those early morning alarms
that failed to wake us up,
Those amazing yearly events of every club,
All these memories will stay with us forever,
These golden years will be there with us in every
endeavour.

The Journey

She prepares to take flight,
With her dreams within sight,
But one thing slips her mind,
The world isn't always kind.

She has the wings,
And the potential to match the winds,
But the journey has just begun,
And every moment of it will not be fun.

They say there is power in dreams,
Blissfully ignorant of the accompanying laborious screams,
But like stars in her eyes they shine,
These dreams make this journey divine.

On and on she has to go,
Whether met with friend or foe,
Weak she cannot be,
Because of her dream she cannot flee.

As Moments Pass By...

Another year has come to a close,
As always, it's been full of highs and lows,
While some moments made me smile,
Others made me ponder about my life for a while.

A year that was as fast as a roller coaster ride,
Where there was literally no place to hide,
So, it was time to face all my fears,
And often, my eyes become filled with years.

But just as a flower waits for the right time to bloom,
The sun did rise, taking away all the gloom,
And while I confess, this year,
happiness did not alway come my way,
But sometimes, to all kinds of music, you have to sway.

So, while every moment of every year may not be happy,
It does not necessarily mean that your
year is going to be crappy,
In some moments, into many fragments,
your heart may be broken,
Of happiness, it always stores a token.

Dreams

My eyes were full of hope,
With the pressure, I was sure I could cope,
But just as I spread my wings for light,
I came to terms with my actual plight.

For excellence, hope is not the only need,
To other things as well it is important to heed.
Life is at no point easy,
Different colours; sometimes dull and at other times,
bright and breezy.

But to survive, you have to weather the storm,
For in reality, one has to abide by the norm,
In this world with wings, one can fly,
But not without being a little sly.

Everyone wants to touch the stars,
But mostly, dreams leave one with a lot of scars,
And facing adversity, those who are
unable to show fortitude,
Let go of everything and they too leave, without
expressing their gratitude.

However, in their dreams those who retain faith,
Same mistakes they never reiterate,
To them their goal always remains clear,
And leaving behind everything,they proceed to it without any fear.

Loyalty and Betrayal

Not that I loved Caesar less, but I loved Rome more,
A statement from the play Julius Caesar, a play that is a
little too close to this world's core,
Caesar whose heart was pure and absolutely true,
Was stabbed to death by his own friends, of whose
betrayal, he had no clue.

Loyalty is an age-old treasure that has now been lost,
And betrayal seems to have made a place for itself
everywhere, no matter what the cost.
Nowadays, the loyal are considered weak,
And betrayers and conspirators are smart, even though
their statements are bleak.

Today, friends are hard to find,
Without loyalty, the world has almost become blind,
It has now lost the pleasure of trust,
And regaining this pleasure is an absolute must.

Now, one has to carefully look,
For conspiracies and betrayals can no
longer be let off the hook,
The world is hurled towards a change
Is betrayal going to win and will the path of loyalty
completely derange??

Who knows?
But then if loyalty is unwanted, why these shows?
Has the world become so weak, that loyalty
has been lost even at the core,
Or is it just that nobody wants to try anymore?

Thinking about Caesar's story makes me sad,
I don't understand this new fad,
But to accept what is wrong,
We, as people, need to stay strong.

Loyalty and betrayal are not two faces of the same coin,
Only one movement out of the two, one can join.
Some might question loyalty's use,
To answer them, I say it is the only way to
bring the world to a truce.

The Top of the Tower

There's a tower in the area where I stay,
And to it's top I go everyday,
From there, the whole world is within my sight,
And it makes me feel that it is
unreasonable for people to fight.

The top of the tower is my safe haven,
And there, I feel as independent as a raven,
From up there, I can see the world at a glance,
And it feels like I've gone into this beautiful trance.

Whether I go there in broad daylight,
Or even in the darkness of the night,
I feel safe there,
And like, nothing or no one can give me a scare.

When problems threaten to taint my life,
And I feel like I can no longer bear any strife,
That is where I go,
There I can think freely, without knowing
which direction am I heading to.

It is where I feel independent,
and even when the sun begins its descent,
and the moon starts to rise,
Being there makes me feel a little more wise.

Being at the top of the tower,
makes me feel like a blooming flower,
ready to take on the world,
Yet, my vision is partially blurred.

But still every day I go there,
Because finally for the distance I don't care,
At the top of the tower, the world is within reach,
And the convention of society, I have decided to breach.

Introspection

Another name for self reflection,
Within yourself,
when you feel like there's a deep confusion,
What you require is intuition.

Look within your soul,
If you don't, the pressure might finally take its toll,
When your instincts tell you that something's wrong,
It means the request for introspection from
within is strong.

Life,they say,is moving on
But that does not mean forgetting what is already gone,
Within yourself, you need to look,
For sometimes, instead of letting go,
you probably need to tighten the hook.

What is it that you want?
That is not a taunt,
Do you want to move forward or go back?
Establish yourself or keep picking up the slack.

Mistakes might already have been made,
It's okay;In life, one should go through every shade.
Look within yourself because that is where the answers lie.
That will speak for you even after you die.

Denial is easy, acceptance is not,
But trust me, it is always your best shot.
So look within yourself again,
For introspection is a boon, not a bane.

So embrace the occasional sunshine:a ray of hope,
Sometimes being calm and looking within yourself might
be exactly what you need to cope,
So, look within yourself from time to time,
Because sometimes, a little push is just
what you need to shine.

The Light at the End of the Tunnel

There is a light at the end of the tunnel is all I know,
And it continues to glow,
Dim at first, but it is there,
But as I walk towards it, the journey gets queer.

Something gets in my way,
But I don't allow the obstacles to stay,
Because if it blocks out the light,
Of my aim, I might lose sight.

There is a light at the end of the tunnel is all I know,
To get to it, I will go wherever I have to go,
But I will have to be careful and smart,
Overcoming obstacles is just a start.

So I keep on going,
The goal is within reach yet the light doesn't
brighten but the darkness continues growing,
Like the thorns of a cactus,
my conscience gets pricked with doubt,
Yet the fight is still left in me,
so I move forward with a final shout.

But going forward has now become my greatest fear,
Looking behind, there is no one here,
I am all alone,
My confidence no longer has the same tone.

What am I doing?
How long will I keep going?
Alone on this path, where no friend
seems to be there to help,
For a sign, a symbol, some meaning in life, I yelp.

And then I see it, yet again
It finally feels like, I am sane,
So I continue my journey to reach for the stars,
Because I believe you can't move forward
without leaving behind some scars.

I have decided that I will go on and on,
I don't know when I will reach, but be it dusk or dawn,
My steps will not stumble now even
if it requires all my will,
Because the light at the end of the
tunnels continues to glow still.